THE BEGINNER'S GUIDE TO
LABOR ARBITRATION PRACTICE

THE BEGINNER'S GUIDE TO
LABOR ARBITRATION PRACTICE

Tips & Strategies for Improving Your Case

ANDREA L. DOOLEY

ISBN: 978-1-7353283-0-0 (Ebook)
ISBN: 978-1-7353283-1-7 (Paperback)

Foreword

I N EVERY ARBITRATION hearing I've done, as an advocate or as an arbitrator, I've made at least one mistake, usually more. As an advocate, I sometimes brought too few copies of my exhibits. I was sometimes too flustered after an objection to find a new way to ask a new question. My supervising partner told me once, after observing me do a hearing, that I touched my hair too often. More than once as an arbitrator, I've fumbled the oath I was administering to a witness. Even worse, I've forgotten to check the address of the hearing location before I left home, resulting in awkward phone calls to advocates and driving around small towns I'd never heard of before.

Just as often, I've also done at least one thing that felt effective and successful in each hearing. It's rarely the same thing twice. I learn from my mistakes and my successes, trying to improve no matter how many hearings I do.

I have also learned from the mistakes and successes of other people. I wrote this book because I wanted to share the best and worst practices I've seen in more than twenty years of labor arbitration and to help newer advocates learn more quickly than I did how to do an arbitration hearing.

While I have an altruistic reason for writing this guide, I also have a selfish reason to share my thoughts. I hope my suggestions will improve the quality and efficiency of labor arbitration. It can be difficult to sit through cases with unprepared advocates. I don't like to see resources spent on a drawn-out hearing that would have the same outcome in an expedited procedure. I want labor arbitration to return to its roots as an efficient and cost-effective way of resolving workplace disputes.

I've made the suggestions in this book to start a conversation about the best and worst of labor arbitration. These suggestions may have application in other alternative dispute forums, but they are grounded in labor arbitration. Practitioners in other areas may consider how my suggestions could be adapted to their practice, but the distinction will be clear.

Despite the title, I didn't just write this book for beginners. Journey level advocates are invited to go back to the basics, fill in the gaps in their knowledge, or just find ideas to disagree with. I've tried to make this guide readable, interesting, and thought-provoking.

Rather than name any specific union or employer in my hypothetical examples, my generic union will be called Thinking Fellers Union Local 282 (or just Local 282) and my generic employer will be called Kraftwerk. In reality, both are highly regarded music bands from my youth and are unrelated to labor arbitration, as far as I know.

The information in this book does not, and is not intended to, constitute legal advice. My thoughts and ideas are for general informational purposes only. Readers should contact their own attorneys to obtain advice about any legal matter. The views expressed in this book are solely my opinion in my individual capacity as the author.

I welcome your thoughts, ideas, and reactions. Please email me at andrealdooley@gmail.com.

Contents

CHAPTER 1
Why Does Labor Arbitration Exist?

General Principles of Grievance and Arbitration

LABOR ARBITRATION IS a form of alternative dispute resolution that is unique to the unionized workplace. While arbitration has grown in popularity among corporations and other legal entities as a way of enforcing contracts, labor arbitration grew out of the Labor Movement and is the final step in a non-judicial grievance framework created by unions and employers.

Without a union contract, every term and condition of employment is set by the employer, subject to federal, state, and local law. When workers have a union, that dynamic shifts. In negotiations, the parties make concessions to change the terms and conditions of employment in the workplace. Unions call these "take-aways." Every term in a labor agreement is one that the Union has helped set, reducing, or even taking away, management's authority over that issue. For example, without a union, the employer has sole discretion to set wages, deny vacation requests, or terminate an employee for no reason. After the parties negotiate a contract, the employer must follow whatever terms they have agreed to, like seniority rules for bidding on vacation use or just cause for discipline. This means the union has "taken away" the employer's discretion on this issue.

Unions rarely have to make concessions in their first contract. The only exceptions to this principle are the grievance procedure and the no-strike clause, two concessions that the Union makes. The traditional way that a union grieves a workplace problem is to withhold labor, also known as going on strike. By agreeing to a grievance procedure and a no-strike clause, a union agrees not to hold a strike or take other labor action that deprives the employer of its labor and instead agrees to resolve disputes within the grievance procedure. The grievance procedure "takes away" the union's right to strike. To ensure labor peace and stability, there is a strong incentive to use the grievance procedure, up through arbitration.

The grievance procedure comes with its own requirements. Instead of walking off the job or going "tools down," as they say in other countries, the union's issue must be stated clearly (usually in writing) and have some basis in the contract, the practices in that workplace, or the law. The grievance must be handled in a manner consistent with the agreed-to process. The benefit to the employer is that disputes are contained, and business can otherwise go on as usual. The benefit to the union is that there is a process that can be used to resolve disputes without having to walk off the job, even if it takes longer than a work stoppage might.

Optimally, grievances are resolved, or "adjusted," at the level closest to the source of the dispute, and only escalate if that doesn't work. When a dispute cannot be resolved between a supervisor and an employee, a union steward or union staff member will intercede on the employee's behalf to resolve it with the supervisor or their manager. If it isn't resolved at that level, the grievance makes its way up the corporate ladder on the steps of the grievance procedure.

Eventually, the union and the employer will agree to disagree, using the final step of the grievance procedure for a final and binding resolution. The parties select a neutral third party to make a decision. Arbitrators fill that role now, but in the past, any "neutral" party could be selected. Clergy members, town elders, and elected officials were conscripted to resolve labor disputes. The common characteristic of an "arbiter" was their trustworthiness to both sides of the dispute. The union and the employer needed to believe not only that the neutral party had their best interest at heart, but also that resolving the dispute in a manner most favorable to both parties was preferable.

We've moved away from that idealized community member who could step in, as in a movie from the 1940s, to soothe over the passions of both the company and the workers with a few considered words of wisdom. Nevertheless, the core principle of selecting a neutral arbiter remains. The parties still want trustworthiness from arbitrators and want fair outcomes that are considerate of both parties' interests and arguments.

For many unions and employers, a grievance that has gotten all the way to arbitration is either a failure of labor relations or exceedingly complex. Most arbitrators understand that they must balance the seriousness of the dispute with the parties' desire for a quick and favorable resolution and that they were selected for their trustworthy and fair nature.

Before we get to arbitration itself, let's talk about the grievance procedure in greater detail.

Practice Tips

- The Grievance Procedure is a "take-away" from the union intended to resolve workplace disputes without work stoppages or labor unrest.
- Grievances should be resolved at the level closest to the source, if possible, but are escalated through the grievance procedure, up to arbitration, if necessary.
- Arbitrators are selected for their trustworthiness and fairness, and arbitrators take their obligation to resolve the parties' dispute very seriously.

CHAPTER 2
The Grievance Procedure

Steps of the Grievance Procedure

EVERY CONTRACT HAS its own grievance procedure with different steps and timelines. The most important part of this process is knowing what your own grievance procedure says, preferably before you need it. I suggest that parties review the grievance procedure and any other applicable language every time they need to use it. This is a point that you should adopt as your mantra: **Read the Contract.**

Despite the differences from contract to contract, grievance procedures do share some common features: steps and timelines.

Steps

Each step of the grievance procedure has a different purpose. The first step is the least formal, and it usually just entails raising the issue to a front line supervisor. It's important to capture what the grievance is, even if it's just memorializing a verbal conversation. An employee's note on their grievance might read: "May 6 – called supv. and let him know my check was short overtime for April 27-28. He said he'll look into it."

Arbitrators aren't strict about whether the exact contract language at issue was cited perfectly, but the dispute should be clearly stated, as it will be a road map for the rest of the process. At the first step—an employee raising an issue to their supervisor—the grievance doesn't need to refer to specific contract sections. The point is to demonstrate that the supervisor learned about the problem.

The example I provided above is a contract dispute. Discipline grievances are almost always filed at the written stage, which will be Step 1 or Step 2, depending on the agreement.

The best case scenario is that the manager or supervisor adjusts the grievance, which means that the dispute is resolved. If it isn't, and the grievance is denied or ignored, it moves to the second step. In some cases, the collective bargaining agreement may indicate that this is the level where the grievance is put in writing. Again, specificity and detail in both the grievance and its response will provide a road map for the rest of the case. Here is a sample: "This email serves as notice that Local 282 disputes the denial of OT for Suzy Banshee on April 27 and 28. She was required to stay 30 minutes past her shift to move boxes. This is a violation of Article 9 of the CBA."

Step 2 in the grievance process is filed with a higher level of management or, occasionally, with the human resources department. Again, the agreement itself will specify where this grievance is directed. During this stage, both parties are gathering information that they will later use at arbitration. Collect documents and note where they came from. Gather witness statements and make sure you get personal contact information for witnesses.

At a Step 2 meeting, the parties should exchange as much information as they can. The purpose of the grievance procedure is to resolve disputes at the lowest possible level, so trying to play "gotcha" by withholding information is strongly disfavored. The employer is legally obligated to provide most information.

If one party believes that relevant information exists but was not provided at Step 2, they should make a request for information. Occasionally, the party in control of the documents, usually the employer, requests a document request. There are several reasons they might reject the request:

1. The request is too broad, asking for records that span a long time frame, are voluminous or difficult to access, or constitute a "fishing expedition;"
2. The request seeks attorney-client privileged materials or documents created for the purpose of bargaining;
3. The request seeks other confidential information.

If there are confidentiality concerns, the parties might agree to just show the information to the union representative or agree to a gag order preventing the information from being shared elsewhere. Medical records and peace officer records (in California) have additional protections under the law, but the union is entitled to them on a need-to-know basis in order to evaluate the merits of the grievance.

Parties have a couple ways of getting information in these instances. You can either file an unfair labor practice charge or subpoena the documents in connection with the arbitration. In that instance, you won't be able to review the documents until the subpoena has been enforced or complied with, which makes it difficult when documents are needed to evaluate the merits of the grievance.

Occasionally one party refuses to disclose the name of a witness. For example, two women complain that their coworker tells jokes of a sexual nature and comments on their body parts but tell the HR compliance manager that they don't want their names used in the complaint or shared with the union. If the employer doesn't disclose these witnesses, it's difficult for the union to investigate the claims and impossible for the arbitrator to rely on their statements when considering the case. Witnesses who prize confidentiality could be disclosed to the union under a similar gag rule as described above, but if the witnesses won't testify at the hearing, the employer has a difficult task proving just cause.

Step 2 is also the time to raise any defenses either party might have. If you fail to raise a defense at this stage, you may find that you've waived that defense later in the case. For example, an employer's defenses might include arguments like 1) the contract doesn't apply (substantive argument), 2) the grievance isn't timely (procedural argument), 3) Suzy clocked out at her regular time and hung around the breakroom for 30 minutes (factual argument). The other party will have to address these issues later in the grievance procedure. The idea is for both parties to put all their cards on the table in the belief that transparency assists in resolution.

The same advice applies to Step 3, which is often the final step before arbitration. At this point, both sides should have a good grasp of the facts and arguments and should have documented each step, all arguments that were made, and new evidence that was shared. Some agreements have mandatory mediation at this point in the process, or they may have a grievance board that reviews the case. Some unions decide whether to take a case to arbitration by presenting it to a grievance committee of their own members. Each of these processes require the parties to know what the facts of the case are, what the arguments are for each side, and have articulated a remedy, which I will discuss later.

Timelines

Each step will have a time frame in which the matter must be moved to the next level, or it will be considered dropped. It's important that the grievance be moved through the steps in a timely fashion. The first time requirement is usually filing the grievance. Grievances need to be filed within a specified time frame of when the union or employee knew or should have known about the alleged contract violation. Sometimes the time limit is as short as five days, sometimes it's as long as thirty days. Knowing the timeline before a violation occurs is critical.

It's rare for a contract to be silent on timing, but occasionally "a reasonable time frame" is the expectation in the agreement. This kind of vague language leads to more disputes, and if one party claims the other didn't act "reasonably," be prepared to justify your position to an arbitrator.

If there's some delay that prevents moving the grievance to the next level, it's a good idea to get agreement in writing from the other side that the timeline is met or waived. Some contracts have very short timelines, requiring an employer to respond within three or five days. If the parties are discussing settlement, or conducting an investigation, one or the other should ask for the deadline to be extended, and if the other side refuses, move the grievance to the next step even while the investigation or settlement discussions are underway.

There is value for both parties in waiving timelines when it is reasonable to do so because it promotes better labor relations and may result in cases being settled more easily or at a lower step in the grievance procedure. This logic applies to be both requests for extensions and untimely grievances.

Here's a hypothetical: Cindy Pauper is a relatively new employee at Kraftwerk, Inc. From the employer's perspective, she's had a terrible absenteeism problem, racking up twenty (20) unexcused absences in just fourteen months on the job. The supervisor, Paul Abdul, sends her a notice of suspension and leaves a copy in the union steward's box, and Cindy leaves the union steward a voicemail saying she wishes to grieve her suspension. The union steward, Adam Aunt, was on vacation. By the time he gets back to work, the seven-day timeline for filing a grievance has passed. Adam asks Paul for a brief extension so he can write a grievance, and Paul agrees. Eventually, the grievance goes to arbitration. The HR Director argues that the grievance was untimely because it was filed more than seven days after the letter of suspension was delivered and that the supervisor had no authority to agree to extend the timeline.

Here are two outcomes I can envision:

1. The arbitrator agrees with management, finds the grievance untimely, and dismisses it. Cindy sues Local 282 for breaching their duty of fair representation. Even though the union prevails in court because they agree that Cindy was absent too often, the union stewards become sticklers about the contract, grieving every problem in sight and never settling anything. The supervisor leaves for another employer because he feels undermined by the HR Director.

2. The arbitrator disagrees with management, finding that if the supervisor had the authority to impose the discipline and adjust grievances at the first level, he has the authority to waive the timeline for filing the grievance. The arbitrator then denies the grievance because the employer demonstrated that they had just cause to suspend Cindy for her absenteeism. The union continues to be amenable to resolving disputes, and the steward and supervisor are able to resolve most issues without any grievances being filed.

This hypothetical shows why occasional leniency on the timelines can be beneficial. On the other hand, both sides need assurances that disputes won't drag on indefinitely, so as a practical matter, extensions should be rare and unnecessary. In practice, you want to avoid arguing about whether the grievance was filed on time and all the deadlines were met. It's much easier to meet the deadlines than ask for an extension.

The purpose of labor relations is to resolve disputes at the lowest level. Arbitrators try to facilitate or improve that relationship. Often arbitrators say that they "abhor forfeiture," meaning that they prefer to reach the substance of the matter, rather than dismissing it on procedural grounds. I will discuss this further in the chapter on arbitrability.

Practice Tips

- READ THE CONTRACT.
- No, seriously, read your contract. You should know what the grievance procedure is before you need to read it. Read it again when you think there's a contract violation. Some people keep a copy of their contract in the bathroom and read a section each time they visit.
- Document the problem, when it gets raised, and the response.
- Mind the timelines in the grievance procedure and follow them. The best practice is to add the steps to your calendar and to-do list.
- If you can, occasionally waive the timelines when there's a really good reason to do so. It's good for long-term labor relations and may result in a speedier resolution of the grievance.

CHAPTER 3
Should I Take the Grievance to Arbitration?

B Y THE TIME the grievance has moved to the arbitration step, the parties are pretty firm that their view of the case is the correct one. It's unlikely that both sides are correct. Once the steps of the grievance procedure have been met, it's important to decide whether this grievance should really go to arbitration. Here are the factors that influence this decision.

Cost

There's an obvious economic cost to arbitration. The parties pay the arbitrator's fees for hearing the case and writing the decision. The parties may retain a court reporter and pay for transcripts. Many times, parties hire outside lawyers. There is a soft cost to the lost productivity that happens when witnesses need to be interviewed and for time spent preparing the case. Those are the costs incurred before the employer has to reckon with the remedy costs if they lose.

Time

Unless the parties take measures to ensure that the matter is heard and decided promptly, arbitration can take longer than the parties hope. From the perspective of a disciplined grievant, the long time frame is frustrating and demoralizing. For the employer, the growing cost of a potential back pay award is daunting. In contract cases, the parties may find themselves in bargaining for a new contract before the matter is even heard. When this happens, the parties should discuss all open grievances at the bargaining table to see whether settlement is possible in the context of a new agreement.

Other Litigation

Effect on Other Grievances

An arbitration decision becomes a part of the contract. Therefore, it will have an effect on other disputes. This can be a good thing or a bad thing. It's good when an arbitrator resolves a dispute that clears up a long-simmering problem, reducing future grievances by clarifying the contract. It's not good when an arbitrator rules so firmly against you that you need to contend with "bad language," meaning language that deepens the dispute, for all your other grievances related to that area. In litigation, it's often said that bad cases make bad law, and that is the case with grievances as well. Think through the impact of a bad decision on your organization's long-term goals. Subsequent arbitrators are often bound by the prior arbitration award when it concerns the same language in the agreement.

Fear of other litigation

Unions must take into consideration their duty of fair representation to their members, and employers should be aware that this duty may compel unions to take a case to arbitration that the employer believes lacks any merit. The duty of fair representation means that a union must fairly represent each member. That doesn't mean they have to take every grievance to arbitration. It means that the basis of the decision not to take a case to arbitration has to be based on the substantive merits of the case and not an administrative snafu. A union can even make an error in judgment about the substantive merits of the case and not be held liable for violating the duty.

The union, on the other hand, may be held responsible if they make an administrative error in handling the grievance that results in the matter not going to arbitration. For example, if a union blows a timeline and the grievance is dismissed as untimely, the grievant may try to recover the lost wages and benefits from the union in federal court. However, a union can decide not to take a grievance to arbitration if they believe the grievance lacks merit. In short, the union must have a reason for withdrawing a grievance. I want to emphasize that there is no duty to take every case to arbitration. Employers should be aware of this consideration even if the union can't tell them about it.

On the flip side, employers are often concerned that aggrieved employees intend to sue them for discrimination or for state law claims. When there is a collective bargaining agreement (or other contract) that requires arbitration, the employer may insist on pursuing discipline within the grievance procedure in an attempt to prevent litigation.

Merits of the Case

The biggest consideration in deciding whether to take a case to arbitration is the merits of the case. In other words, will you win? As soon as the parties decide to arbitrate, it's a very good idea for both sides to make a list of the union's and the employer's arguments and note the evidence needed to support or refute that argument. Who are the witnesses? Will they testify willingly? Do you have all the documents you need, or do you need to do an information request?

Evaluating the merits of a grievance is one of the more difficult tasks a new practitioner faces when they get their first arbitration case. Here's an example of the type of analysis that could be written by either side, with the evidence to support it noted in parentheses:

Employer's Arguments	Union's Arguments
Video evidence of employee sleeping (video)	Employee admitted the behavior (employee testimony)
Supervisor witnessed employee and woke him (supervisor testimony)	Employee apologized (employee testimony)
Second time this has happened (documentation of prior discipline)	Employee is a 26-year employee (stipulated)
Clear work rules prohibit sleeping on the shop floor (documentation of rule and showing employee knew of rule)	He was resting his eyes during his break and inadvertently napped briefly. Slept in the breakroom, not on the shop floor (time records show he did clock out for his break)

Too often, arbitrators see advocates who are not prepared for arguments the other side raises, or who make arguments that have no basis in fact. Preparing for arbitration early in the grievance process will either save you the expense of a difficult losing case or will help you prepare a stronger, more winning case.

Imagine you have made the notes above. It would be very hard to conclude from those arguments whether you would win the case or not, and it will probably proceed to arbitration. In a lot of cases, however, taking the time to evaluate the merits of your case can help you decide whether to proceed to arbitration. It may also help you see a path to settlement, or even convince you to grant or withdraw the grievance. Even if it does not, your notes will be valuable when it comes to preparing for the hearing itself.

Being Prepared

The reason I advise doing this analysis as soon as you move to arbitration is because you can revisit the analysis in three or six months— or whenever you go to arbitration—and see if anything has changed. Your best witness might have been fired. The grievant may have moved. A month before hearing, you look at your notes and realize that the supervisor is gone and won't testify, or that the employee now denies that it was him sleeping in the breakroom. These changes might cause you to reevaluate your chances of winning and thus influence your willingness to present the case to an arbitrator. Even if the evidence is still available, you or your attorney will be glad you wrote yourself a road map when the case was fresh.

Remedy

The remedy is the outcome granted by the arbitrator as part of their decision. In arbitration, remedies are limited to what you would have gotten if the contract had not been violated. Unlike civil litigation, there are no punitive damages, for example. When evaluating a case, it's important to ask what you want from the case and what you can reasonably expect to win. It also helps to ask yourself what outcome you can expect if you lose.

It might be possible that the parties could reach a better outcome with a settlement than with an arbitrator's award. For the union, a Last Chance Agreement (LCA) or a resignation for a discharged employee might be a better outcome than losing the case. For management, reinstatement of an employee with a lesser discipline might be better now than a year from now, when the back pay and benefits costs have started to mount. In other words, the parties should evaluate whether there is an acceptable outcome that is short of losing and short of winning.

In evaluating the remedy, the parties might conclude the remedy has little value. For example, if the grievant is employed elsewhere and not interested in returning to work, arbitration might not be necessary to resolve the grievance. On the other hand, an employed grievant may be under less pressure to settle, and the employer faces less exposure in back pay. Sometimes, in evaluating the remedy, you realize there's no monetary value, and you'd be better off deferring the matter to bargaining. Knowing what you want from the grievance procedure is almost as important as knowing if you'll win.

So, what can you win? When I represented unions, I often told individual employees not to expect "justice" from the arbitrator. The arbitrator wasn't going to make someone apologize or award damages for pain and suffering. Arbitrators are limited to contract remedies, which are "make whole," meaning you can get what you would have gotten if the contract hadn't been violated.

If you are the employer, the remedy you hope for is the status quo. You want the arbitrator to confirm that you had just cause to terminate an employee or that you didn't violate the contract when you mandated overtime work. In some cases, employers will request attorney's fees or an order requiring the union to pay all the costs of arbitration. Arbitrators rarely grant these requests unless there's a contract provision or extraordinary circumstances, like the union caused delay using some bad faith tactics.

Unions have a wider array of contract remedies available. In a disciplinary case, the Union may seek reinstatement, a lower level of discipline, back pay with interest, and all lost benefits. In a contract case, Unions want contract enforcement, injunctive relief, and for their members to be made whole monetarily. Unions may also occasionally ask for attorney's fees and arbitration costs. Again, they are rarely awarded unless there is explicit contract language or bad faith conduct by the employer.

It's important to identify the remedy you seek at the time you are evaluating the case. It may help settlement, either early on or later, when you prepare for arbitration. It's also important to articulate to the arbitrator what remedy you seek. Arbitrators who don't have that road map may craft remedies that neither party wants.

Arbitrators will also occasionally craft novel remedies, like completion of drug rehabilitation or a Last Chance Agreement as a condition of returning an employee to work in a discipline case. In cases where it's difficult to know which employees were harmed, but a deterrence message is sought, the Arbitrator might order a contribution to an education fund or apprenticeship program in the industry. The parties don't usually request these remedies, and many people feel that they go beyond the scope of the arbitrator's authority but be aware that they occur. The parties may even agree beforehand to tell the arbitrator what they believe is not acceptable.

Practice Tips

- Document the best arguments of both the union and the employer.
- Identify your remedy.
- Consider the costs and time involved and determine whether they are worth the remedy you seek.

CHAPTER 4
Selecting an Arbitrator

T HE PROCESS OF selecting an arbitrator is often laid out in the agreement. There are several different ways that contracts specify arbitrator selection.

Permanent Panel in the Agreement: Rotation from a list

Some Collective Bargaining Agreements (CBAs) list a permanent panel of individual arbitrators that the parties rotate through their cases. Rotation means that you do not have to worry about selecting an arbitrator—whichever one is next in rotation will have your case. For example, Local 282's contract says: "The parties will select an arbitrator from among the following names; Fred, Wilma, Barney, Betty, Bam Bam." For many years, Kraftwerk and Local 282 rotated through the arbitrators in order; the first grievance would go to Fred, the second to Wilma, and so on. After many years, Kraftwerk decided Barney was too pro-union, and Local 282 hated an award that Wilma wrote. That left Fred, Betty, and Bam Bam to hear arbitration cases.

It is worth giving feedback to the contract negotiators if you have a very bad or very good experience with an arbitrator, so the negotiator knows whether to try to keep them or replace them on the list. The arbitrator panel in the agreement is rarely as important as the wage negotiations, but it does have a big impact over the life of the Agreement. Keep that list current. It's shocking how many agreements mention arbitrators who are no longer working.

Arbitration Services or Arbitration Rosters

Some agreements specify that the parties will use lists provided by a roster service, such as the American Arbitration Association (AAA), the Federal Mediation and Conciliation Service (FMCS), or their state public employment relations board. The roster service websites make it very easy to get randomly generated lists of arbitrators and will provide lists of arbitrators with specific expertise or in a particular region. Some arbitration services are "full service" and will do scheduling and other administrative functions.

Some contracts also have a list of arbitrators available for selection. Talk to colleagues about their experiences with the arbitrators on the list. Arbitrators may not be viewed as wholly good or bad. Some may be favorable on discipline cases but bad on cases involving back wages. If you are selecting an arbitrator where you are "striking names," don't start with your most objectionable. If there are five names, rank them according to your preference. You will strike two names, and the other side will strike two names. You want to make sure that the arbitrators you ranked #4 and #5 are struck. First round, strike the less objectionable (#4). It is possible that the other side will strike your most objectionable, and you will be able to strike #3 with your second round.

Ad Hoc or Private Selection

When the contract is silent, the parties might suggest arbitrators to one another until there's agreement. It's common to gravitate to the names you recognize, or, more commonly, shy away from the names of arbitrators who have ruled against you in the past. People stay away from unfamiliar names, which is too bad. More established arbitrators are harder to schedule. A few arbitrators I know do not have available dates for up to a year in the future. Relying on a small pool of arbitrators often means new arbitrators with more diverse backgrounds have a difficult time establishing a practice. This leads to complaints from practitioners that there aren't enough diverse arbitrators or arbitrators who are available to hear a case on short notice.

If you would like to see a more diverse group of arbitrators, propose the names of newer arbitrators to the other party and see if they're interested. When I first started practicing, I was picked with some frequency by two parties I had no previous knowledge of. After our third hearing, the lawyers both told me (together) that they had originally selected me because, for one reason or another, they'd rejected every other arbitrator on several lists they received!

It's understandable that parties want to know what kinds of decisions they can expect. Established arbitrators are more likely to offer consistency in that regard. There are useful ways to evaluate new arbitrators.

1. Read their resume: The best indicator that a new arbitrator will be familiar with labor arbitration is that they have experience with collective bargaining, contract administration, and grievance handling. General employment law or human resources experience isn't helpful unless it was in a unionized work environment.

2. Review their training: While it isn't foolproof, if an arbitrator has completed the FMCS Becoming an Arbitrator training or an analogous National Academy of Arbitrators or state training, they should have a good grounding in the basics. The FMCS course includes a decision writing assignment (the "Nurse Kevin" case). You can request a copy of that work as a writing sample if the arbitrator doesn't have any published decisions available.

3. Ask your colleagues: Although your colleagues may seem like a great source of information, take their feedback with a grain of salt, since a losing party might be more negative than necessary. You might ask the colleague if you can read the award they received. What you want to know is: can they run a hearing, make clear evidentiary rulings, and manage the whole case efficiently? Is the arbitrator fair, and what does fair mean to your colleague? Do they express their opinions in a clear and readable way that your staff and/or membership will understand? Employers occasionally rely on a service called Simpsons, which writes reports on arbitrators. The union-side

bar has a less formal approach to sharing information but are forthcoming with their opinions when asked. I believe that the AFL-CIO Lawyers Coordinating Committee may have a listserv for its members where lawyers can find arbitrator recommendations.

Still not sure you are ready to trust someone new? Some parties who have multiple grievances pending agree to hire a new arbitrator to mediate a set of grievances. The parties pick 3-6 grievances and do oral presentations to the arbitrator, who then tries to help settle the cases. If they are unable to settle the cases, the arbitrator might offer a non-binding advisory opinion. The upside to this approach for the parties is the exposure to the arbitrator's approach to cases, possible settlement of grievances, and a non-binding third-party opinion that may influence the parties' positions on the case. There isn't really a downside except for the expense of the arbitrator's per diem expense. Still, six cases for the price of one isn't a bad deal.

Everyone has seen a resume before. The purpose of the resume is to provide information about an individual's personal experience, skills, and background. An arbitrator's work history will tell you whether they have relevant experience in collective bargaining and labor relations, and whether they have any specialized knowledge. If an arbitrator formerly worked for a pension fund, it would indicate they have extensive experience in ERISA and Taft-Hartley Trust Funds. My employment as a Safety Leader gives me a firsthand understanding of occupational safety and health issues.

When reading an arbitrator's resume, the parties should be looking for more than just their experience. Read the resume as a disclosure document as well. Arbitrators cannot anticipate what matters or associations might create a doubt in the mind of one of the parties. Their resume is the first effort to inform parties about the matters and associations they've had.

Commercial arbitrators have a duty to disclose any "all matters that could cause a person aware of the facts to reasonably entertain a doubt that the proposed neutral **arbitrator** would be able to be impartial." Cal. Code Civ. Proc. § 1982.9(a). FMCS, NAA and

AAA share a Code of Professional Responsibility for Arbitrators that provides more thorough guidance about disclosure for labor arbitrators (https://naarb.org/code-of-professional-responsibility/).

The disclosure rules for labor arbitrators are different from arbitrators in commercial cases. Labor Arbitrators don't have to disclose every professional contact they've had with the parties or their representatives, but they do need to disclose personal relationships. It's commonly understood among labor practitioners that arbitrators have had other cases with one or both parties in the past, and that not every case needs to be disclosed. The reason for this is that arbitrators are better able to facilitate long-term, mature labor relations if they have a deeper knowledge of the contracts and industries in which they hear cases. This is unique to labor arbitration, and the disclosure requirements for other arbitrators are much stricter.

Look at the arbitrator's work history. Anyone can see that I worked at a labor law firm for over a decade ago and then worked for a major local hospital chain. Those are disclosures that might inform parties considering me for selection.

Labor arbitrators do disclose personal relationships. For example, during a recent hearing, I learned that the Human Resources Director, who was not present, was a parent of a child at my son's school. I disclosed the connection even though we had no personal or social relationship and neither side seemed to care. I prefer to err on the side of disclosure because if someone later learned of the connection, they might conclude I hid the information for some reason, and I don't want them to draw that conclusion.

Another area to explore is the arbitrator's publications list, if they have one. While most decisions are confidential, a few arbitrators do seek to publish their decisions, which can help the parties understand how an arbitrator approaches issues. Articles and other scholarly contributions can also help the parties gain insights into an arbitrator's mindset.

Arbitrators who appear at conferences are always willing to answer questions at those events, as long as they aren't about a case that is pending before them. Take the opportunity to introduce yourself to arbitrators you meet at professional events and ask a question or two.

I've included a mock resume as a sample so you can practice reviewing resumes.

Polly Mathis, Arbitrator
900 W. Broadway # 72
Clayton, CA 95555
(510) 555-3089
www.notarealwebsite.com

PROFESSIONAL EXPERIENCE

2014-present: Arbitrator (grievance and arbitrations, fact-finding hearings, civil service hearings, mediation, labor-management partnerships, interest-based bargaining)

2011-2014: Director of Safety, St. Marie's Hospital, Oakland, California

2009-2011: Business Representative, Coalition of Healthcare Worker Unions, Vacaville, California

2005-2008: Partner, Van and Borg Law Firm, Oakland, California

2000-2005: Associate, Van and Borg Law Firm, Oakland, California

EDUCATIONAL BACKGROUND

JD, University of California, Boalt Hall, 2000
BA, University of Chicago, 1996

ADMISSION TO PRACTICE LAW

State of California, 2000; United States District Courts, California, 2000; United States Court of Appeals, Ninth Circuit, 2000 (SBN: 222222)

PUBLIC SERVICE

2019-present: President, Clayton High School Parent Teacher Student Association, Clayton, California

2017-2018: Commissioner, Solano County Environmental Protection Commission, Solano, California

PANELS

Alameda County Transit and Amalgamated Transit Union, American Arbitration Association, AAA Tribal Labor Panel, California State Mediation and Conciliation Service, California Public Employment Relations Board, Panel of Neutrals, California State University and California Faculty Association, County of Los Angeles Civil Service Commission, Communication Workers of America District 9 and AT&T West, County of Los Angeles Employment Relations Commission, Equal Employment Opportunity Commission Federal Mediation Program, Federal Mediation and Conciliation Service, Los Angeles Employee Relations Board, National Mediation Board, United States Postal Service and American Postal Workers Union, AFL-CIO Arbitration Panel, Washington Public Employment Relations Commission

INDUSTRIES

Transportation (rail, public transit), freight, healthcare, entertainment, communications, professional and technical, building trades, service industries, public sector, education, higher education, cities and counties, law enforcement, postal, and service.

MEMBERSHIPS

California State Bar, CLA - Labor and Employment Section, Bar Association of San Francisco, BASF ADR and Labor & Employment Sections, Orange County Labor and Employment Relations and Research Association

PUBLICATIONS AND OTHER ACTIVITIES

"Technology and Ethics: A Guide for Neutrals," ABA <u>Just Resolutions</u> Newsletter, March 2015.

<u>DHL Express and Teamsters</u>, 135 LA 1858 (2016)

<u>YRC Freight and Teamsters</u>, 136 LA 50 (2016)

<u>DHL Express and Teamsters</u>, 139 LA 653 (2019)

Faculty, Labor Arbitration Institute

Program Chair, 2017 "Meet the Arbitrator" Conference, National Academy of Arbitrators, Northern California Region

It's easy to find out how much an arbitrator will charge. Arbitrators publish rate schedules, and these can be obtained directly from the arbitrator simply by asking. Some arbitrators post their rates on their websites. You can also obtain an arbitrator's resume and rate schedule from the agencies that provide arbitrator rosters (AAA and FMCS, for example).

Arbitrators usually charge by the day (called a per diem rate). A "day" is typically up to eight hours for a hearing. Some arbitrators specify that they will charge a second "day" if the hearing exceeds eight hours.

Arbitrator's per diem rates vary throughout the country. The Federal Mediation and Conciliation Service publishes an annual survey of per diem rates. Don't judge an arbitrator on their per diem rate alone. Some charge a low rate but drag out the hearing or take a long time to write a report. While this conduct is rare (and possibly unethical), one arbitrator in New York City made the news when he charged more than a hundred hours on a case that had a one-day hearing. Most arbitrators would have written a decision in a couple of days.

Arbitrators are split on how they charge for studying the record and writing a decision. Some charge another full "day" for each day of study and writing, while other arbitrators charge a pro-rated fee. An arbitrator might charge $2400 for the hearing day and then $300 per hour for study and writing, while another arbitrator charges $2400 for up to eight hours of study and writing.

Arbitrators charge for travel expenses, including airfare, cabs/ rideshare rides, hotels, trains, mileage, and tolls. Their rate schedule will specify limitations for travel. Some arbitrators may require the purchase of a refundable plane ticket or first class passage if the trip will take longer than three hours. Many arbitrators also charge a pro-rated travel time if a trip will exceed a certain time or distance from their home. For example, I charge for travel time if the round trip will take more than two hours.

One of the most important parts of the arbitrator's rate schedule is the cancellation fee, which is the cost the parties will incur if they do not cancel or reschedule the hearing within a certain time frame. Cancellation times vary widely among arbitrators and can be confusing, particularly about whether the arbitrator considers business days or calendar days. A good practice I've seen parties use is to send the chosen arbitrator a message that confirms the hearing date and the cancellation date. For an arbitrator with a 30-day cancellation period, the language would state: "This will confirm that the hearing date for this matter is March 26, 2020. It's our understanding that the cancellation date for this matter is February 25, 2020. If that is not correct, please let us know."

Arbitrator per diem rates don't vary widely within regions. Some areas of the country don't have enough work for arbitrators to do only labor cases, while other regions do. After you've seen a few arbitrator rate schedules, you'll get a sense of what the range is in your area. Arbitrators who do employment cases sometimes charge twice what labor arbitrators charge. Arbitrators who do other types of cases, like commercial arbitrators, tend to charge an even higher rate. Unions have smaller budgets and often avoid arbitrators whose rates exceed the average by a great deal. Obviously, there's a ceiling above which few parties would pay.

When considering an arbitrator for selection, it is more useful to note the expenses an arbitrator charges. Travel expenses and necessary meals are customary; office expenses like calendaring and copying are less customary but happen. Most of all, mind the cancellation fee. Always calendar the date you'll incur a cancellation fee and try to settle or cancel the case before that to avoid incurring a fee you or your client didn't expect. I've included a mock rate schedule as an example.

Sample Rate Schedule

Polly Mathis, Arbitrator
900 W. Broadway # 72
Clayton, CA 95555
(510) 555-3089
www.notarealwebsite.com
Rates for Labor Arbitration, Factfinding,
and Grievance Mediation

The following rates apply for all selections made after March 1, 2019:

Per Diem

The fee is $2,400 per day for each day of hearing. A hearing day is any portion of a day up to eight hours. Time for research and preparation of the Opinion, Award or Report is prorated at an hourly rate of $300 per hour.

Cancellation

If the scheduled hearing is postponed or canceled with notice of less than 21 calendar days, the per diem rate for each day of hearing shall be charged if another cannot be set in its place.

Expenses

There are no charges for routine copying, phone, clerical, or incidental office expenses. Parties are charged for the actual cost of reasonable travel and case-related expenses, including airfare and other transportation (e.g., car rental, parking, taxi), food, and lodging. Automobile mileage is charged at the applicable IRS expense rate for the use of my personal vehicle.

Travel Time

There is no charge for travel time in the Bay Area. If more than two hours of travel time are needed for round trip travel to and from the hearing location, travel time is $200 per hour.

Individual Cases

Cases involving an individual grievant or employee who is not represented by a union or employee organization will require a deposit of the cost of one hearing day prior to scheduling the hearing. The deposit will be applied to any costs incurred by the parties and will be refunded in full if the hearing is canceled 21 calendar days before the scheduled day of hearing.

Practice Tips

- READ THE CONTRACT to find out how arbitrators are selected under this CBA.
- Ensure that your arbitration list is current.
- Read the resumes and rate schedules of new arbitrators and consider selecting someone new.

CHAPTER 5
Arbitration That's Fast, Cheap, and Under Control

Arbitration should be quick and efficient

LABOR ARBITRATION WAS created to avoid the lengthy delays and anti-union bias that was associated with the courts in the early 20th century. The United States Supreme Court's Steelworkers Trilogy confirmed the value of labor arbitration as a labor relations dispute resolution tool in 1961, and arbitration has been the culminating point of grievance procedures ever since.

In theory, arbitration should be a quick and efficient process for resolving grievances, but, in recent years, cases sometimes take as long as litigation does. Speedy arbitration has many benefits to consider. There is less back pay exposure, more likely availability of witnesses and their memories, and quicker resolution of the issue, all of which lead to greater certainty about the "law of the workplace." In other words, the parties get it over with!

There are many ways to streamline or shorten your arbitration case. To resolve grievances more quickly, try these tools:

1. Grievance Mediation: Instead of going straight to arbitration, consider using a mediator from FMCS or your state mediation service to discuss settlement. This can be helpful when one party has fewer resources or believes a settlement could be achieved

with the help of a neutral third party. Many state agencies offer free or low-cost mediation services.

2. Hire an arbitrator by availability: A newer arbitrator offers several benefits that can shorten the length of time to hearing and the cost of the proceeding. Their per diem rates tend to be lower, on average. They have more availability to schedule cases sooner than busier arbitrators, which reduces back pay exposure and ensures quicker resolution. With a lighter caseload, the arbitrator can write a decision more quickly too.

3. Skip the court reporter: In some cases, a transcript is a necessary expense, either because the record is voluminous, the oral testimony is essential, or the arbitrator relies on it for maintaining their own record. If you have very few witnesses, a one-day hearing, and a willing arbitrator, consider doing the case without a court reporter. Non-discharge disciplinary cases or cases with only one or two witnesses are amenable to this approach.

4. Skip the closing brief: Some arbitrators request a written closing brief. Personally, I've only requested one on a few occasions: when we were long past 5 p.m. and everyone was tired, and when a legal issue arose that the parties and I agreed necessitated legal briefs. More often, one or both parties wish to file a written closing brief, and that's fine, too.

I always welcome closing arguments at the hearing in lieu of written briefs. The case is then submitted, and I can start writing a decision. The parties don't have to pay their lawyers to write a brief, and the decision comes that much more quickly.

In some cases in the Bay Area, one party wants to write a closing brief while the other party wishes to do an oral argument. In most cases, the parties won't agree to this split because the oral arguer doesn't want to preview their arguments for the brief writer, and the brief writer doesn't want to leave the oral arguer alone with the arbitrator. There is one exception we use, however. If there's a court reporter present, the party who wants to give an oral closing argument can give it to the court reporter who transcribes it for the record. The other party and the arbitrator are not present for the argument. The court reporter transcribes it as a separate document and sends it to the arbitrator. The arbitrator will provide it to the other side when the brief writer has submitted their brief. This saves one party the expense of a closing brief.

5. Ask for a bench decision: A bench decision is one that the arbitrator "gives from the bench" at hearing, meaning they render a decision after the conclusion of oral arguments but before everyone leaves. This saves the expense of the arbitrator's study and writing fees. If the arbitrator or the parties aren't comfortable with that approach, ask the arbitrator for a summary decision within seven days. A summary decision is similar to a bench decision but in a written format. You should request this from the arbitrator at the time you retain them. Some arbitrators may charge a full day of study and writing, however, so be clear about what you are hoping to do (save money).

6. Streamline and Stipulate: Many practitioners treat the hearing like a full-blown jury trial and prepare as though every single fact or document will be contested by the other side. In reality, very little is in dispute. Many facts can be stipulated. Many documents can be joint exhibits. A short pre-hearing discussion between the advocates can yield a lot of agreement and save time and paper. Here are some examples of facts that can be stipulated: dates, prior discipline, names of witnesses, and locations. Preparing the CBA, grievance file, personnel records, timesheets, policies & procedures, and training materials as joint exhibits also shortens the hearing and shrinks the paper record.

7. Don't Use Lawyers: This suggestion will be unwelcomed by the lawyers reading my book. I'm suggesting that unions and employers could permit staff to present the grievance to the arbitrator, instead of hiring outside counsel. The truth is, experienced staff are just as good at advocating at arbitration as

a lawyer. Staff have a sense of the contract, the history of the parties, and what's really relevant to the case. Using salaried staff is a cost-effective method of doing an arbitration hearing. Both union representatives and human resource specialists can be trained to successfully advocate at hearings.

8. Submit your dispute on the papers: When you submit a dispute "on the papers," it means you are submitting evidence and written briefs to the arbitrator without a hearing or sworn witness testimony. This is particularly successful for arbitrability issues or remedy issues. It saves the cost of the hearing.

9. Arbitrator with a hearing officer: In the past, experienced arbitrators would hire staff to act as hearing officers. Almost unheard of now, the hearing officer would conduct the hearing, make a record, and solicit arguments. The hearing officer would prepare a summary of the facts and might make a recommendation on the outcome but would have no authority to issue a decision. All this would be submitted to the more experienced arbitrator, who would render a final and binding decision on the record compiled by the hearing officer. This is similar to how the National Labor Relations Board and some state labor boards work. Many esteemed arbitrators started out this way. It has largely fallen out of use, which is unfortunate. The arbitrator pays the hearing officer, so there's no additional cost to the parties. The hearing is held, and the decision is rendered much more quickly than if the arbitrator had done the case. The outcome is no different than if she'd done it, and the parties still benefit from the experienced arbitrator's wisdom and expertise. Parties might consider asking an arbitrator to use a hearing officer or take up the offer of an arbitrator who is interested in resuming this practice.

10. Hearing by videoconference: Prior to the COVID-19 pandemic, it was rare to hold a complete hearing by video conference. The technology, when used, was reserved for the occasional witness. As a result of the shelter-in-place orders and concerns about health, arbitrators started developing protocols

for hosting video hearings. While it's not appropriate for every case, video hearings can reduce travel expenses and time without a reduction in quality.

To assist in facilitating video hearings, I trained with other arbitrators to become comfortable "hosting" the hearing and developed a procedure, which I share below, to ensure we had everything we needed for an efficient and confidential hearing.

Andrea L. Dooley, Arbitrator
953 W. MacArthur Blvd. #8
Oakland, CA 94608
(510) 719-3089
www.andreadooleyarbitration.com

VIDEO ARBITRATION HEARING PROCEDURES

1. Please provide the names and cell phone numbers of every participant to the Arbitrator and the party representatives at least one day prior to the hearing.
2. Please provide copies of all documents and/exhibits to the arbitrator, other parties, and witnesses in advance of the hearing. Exhibits should be identified and numbered in advance (such as Union Ex. 1). If additional exhibits are identified during the hearing, they should be emailed to the opposing advocate for review before being presented to the arbitrator or witness.
3. Please join the Zoom at least five minutes prior to your scheduled meeting time to ensure that you are able to access the meeting.
4. Once you have joined the meeting, you will be placed in a waiting room until the host/arbitrator allows you into the meeting. If you are joining the meeting as a claimant or witness, you may need to wait until the parties have finished other business. Please stay on the line.

5. No recording of the proceeding is permitted unless the parties retain a court reporter for that purpose.

6. Once the claimant or witness has joined the meeting and been sworn, they will be asked the following:

   a. To identify any individuals who are present with them in the room;

   b. To put away any notes, documents, photographs, and electronic devices that they may have which are not being used during the course of the hearing;

   c. To confirm they understand that they may not record the proceeding.

7. As in an in-person hearing, all parties, including witnesses and claimants, are reminded to wait until the other party has finished speaking before they begin. Please wait until the arbitrator has ruled on any objections before speaking. Non-witness and non-representative participants will be muted during testimony.

8. Unless there is an agreement between the parties to the contrary, the "chat" function will not be enabled. Side discussions may take place via text messaging; however, at no time can a party representative or witness communicate with another witness during their testimony. Alternately, at the request of the parties, a private chat function can be enabled for the party representatives, but they may not communicate privately with the arbitrator or witness. All chats will be deleted at the end of the hearing.

9. If either party requests a caucus or break, all parties will be put into their own breakrooms.

10. The panel may also request an executive session. At that time, the host will put the panel into a breakroom and the parties into their own separate breakrooms.

11. The parties are invited to confer and let me know if you agree on a modification or enhancement of this procedure.

Practice Tips

To save time and money on arbitration, try these methods:

- Grievance mediation
- Hire available arbitrators
- Don't get a court reporter
- Don't file closing briefs
- Ask for a bench decision
- Stipulate to the facts and file joint exhibits
- Don't use lawyers
- Submit on the papers
- Hire an arbitrator who uses a hearing officer
- Video arbitration hearing

CHAPTER 6
Preparing for the Hearing

General Considerations

O NCE YOU HAVE selected the arbitrator to hear the grievance, it's time to deal with the logistics of the hearing. Both sides need to agree on a date, time, and location for the hearing.

Some arbitrators (or their assistants) will help facilitate the scheduling process. For example, I have an availability calendar on my website that permits the parties to select a hearing date without having to call me. Other arbitrators offer a few dates and let the parties tell them which days they are available. For some reason, selecting a date is one of the most difficult logistical tasks, but it must be done first. If having the hearing done quickly is important to one or both parties, I recommend prioritizing this task.

In the rare cases that one party refuses to agree to a hearing date, the party seeking to schedule the date may ask the arbitrator to set a hearing date and order the parties to appear. Many arbitrators will arrange a conference call with the parties to sort out logistical problems that the parties cannot resolve themselves.

Most hearings are held at either the employer's or the union's office, or at the office of one of their attorneys. Although I've never had an occasion where the parties refused to agree on a location, I know another arbitrator who says, "If the parties cannot agree to a location, then I will schedule a conference room at the Ritz-Carlton with tea service. Expenses will be shared by the parties." She reports that parties are always able to resolve the problem when faced with the prospect of a large bill from the Ritz.

Should you hire a court reporter or not? Whether to use a court reporter varies by region, industry, arbitrator, and parties. I do not require a court reporter. I take copious notes, and they help me concentrate on the case. However, I do prefer a transcript be prepared for cases that extend over multiple days. If I am provided with a transcript, even for a short case for which I have notes, I always refer to it to confirm my recollection of the facts.

With some exceptions, parties with private counsel (that is, outside attorneys) prefer transcripts. This allows them, and their associates who did not attend, to prepare detailed closing briefs. For me, a simple, one-day case rarely needs a transcript, but other arbitrators disagree with me on that. Confirm with your arbitrator what their preferred practice is.

Preparing Documents

Before you start preparing witnesses, pull together all the documents you intend to use as evidence in the case. "Documents" means paper documents and other physical evidence, such as photographs and videos. Original documents are best, but in most cases, readable copies are acceptable. Make sure that the copies you intend to introduce are the same as the originals that were used in the underlying matter. It sounds obvious, but a lot of time can be spent at the hearing trying to decipher notes or alterations to a document that the other side objects to.

By preparing documents before preparing witnesses, you will have time to identify missing documents and locate them either within your organization, from the grievant, from witnesses, or from the other side. In some cases, you may need a subpoena duces tecum for documents the other side won't produce. I'll address subpoenas in the section on Preparing Witnesses.

Once you have your documents in one place, put them in order. The order you choose is up to you. It could be chronological or in the order you intend to call witnesses. Generally, the collective bargaining agreement and grievance are among the first documents. They can usually be joint exhibits, as well as policies, procedures, rules, performance evaluations, grievance correspondence, and anything else both parties intend to introduce as evidence. Talk to the other side about your joint exhibits and decide who will bring those copies. I always appreciate when parties make an effort to reduce the amount of paper I need to bring home. Save the trees!

Now that you have your documents in order, make copies for yourself, the grievant, the other side, the arbitrator (often receives the original), and the witness. That's five (5) copies for the hearing. These are in addition to copies you provide to a witness during prep. Court reporters will often keep the witness set of documents and send them to the arbitrator with the completed transcript. You can number your exhibits, but you don't have to. Here's a sample of the documents in evidence on a typical discipline case.

Joint Exhibit 1 – Collective bargaining agreement
Joint Exhibit 2 – Grievance
Joint Exhibit 3 – Step 2 letter
Joint Exhibit 4 – Step 3 letter
Joint Exhibit 5 – Performance evaluation

Employer's Exhibit 1 – Letter of discharge
Employer's Exhibit 2 – Witness statement
Employer's Exhibit 3 – Timecards
Employer's Exhibit 4 – Prior discipline

Union's Exhibit 1 – Doctor's note
Union's Exhibit 2 – Letters of commendation

Witnesses

Before the hearing, the parties should also come to an agreement about witnesses. Once you know the hearing date, make sure your witnesses know, too. In the best case scenario (or because the contract requires it), the parties identify their witnesses ahead of time and work together to ensure that the witnesses are available on the hearing date. This means releasing witnesses from work to testify, determining pay arrangements, and coordinating subpoenas for witnesses who are reluctant to testify or need a subpoena to be released from work. Subpoenas are also helpful if a witness needs to be excused from jury duty or to reschedule another matter. The parties might also agree that some witnesses will appear by video or telephone, or that a witness's written statement is sufficient.

Arbitrators prefer that parties coordinate on this process because resolving disputes about witnesses at the hearing feels needless, time-consuming, and argumentative. If one party is not willing to cooperate in arranging witnesses, the party calling that witness should request a subpoena from the arbitrator as early as possible.

Arbitrators have different practices on subpoenas. Some want the parties to prepare a subpoena and send it to the arbitrator for signature. Other arbitrators will sign blank subpoenas and let the party requesting them to fill in the details. Still others have their staff to do the entire subpoena itself. Ask the arbitrator what their practice is and do so with enough advance warning that the arbitrator can prepare subpoenas before the hearing, with time to spare for serving the subpoena and for the witness to make arrangements to be available.

Here is the subpoena policy that I share with the parties when they ask:

Subpoena Policy

I will sign subpoenas and/or subpoenas duces tecum requested and prepared by either party with notice to the other side, pursuant to California state law and subject to any applicable terms of the collective bargaining agreement.

Expert Witnesses

Expert witnesses are not as common in labor arbitration as they are in other proceedings, but there are certain kinds of cases that are more likely to warrant expert testimony. One or both parties might call expert witnesses to testify at the hearing in cases involving drug and alcohol use, fitness for duty, standard operating procedures, and handwriting or forgery cases.

Again, in the best case scenario, the parties identify expert witnesses ahead of time so that the other side can prepare their cross-examination and hire their own expert. If the grievance involves one of the issues I identified above, your case may warrant discussing the facts with an expert to see whether, as a layperson, you have misunderstood the other side's rationale. You may conclude that an expert could help your case.

So, who is an expert? Expert witnesses in federal court are held to a high standard set by the Federal Rules. While the federal rules don't apply in arbitration, they are helpful for understanding the difference between a lay witness' opinion and an expert witness. Federal Rule of Evidence 702 states:

A witness who is qualified as an expert by knowledge, skill, experience, training, or education may testify in the form of an opinion or otherwise if:

    a. the expert's scientific, technical, or other specialized knowledge will help the trier of fact to understand the evidence or to determine a fact in issue;

    b. the testimony is based on sufficient facts or data;

    c. the testimony is the product of reliable principles and methods; and

    d. the expert has reliably applied the principles and methods to the facts of the case.

While a layperson may provide their opinion, it isn't "expert." It serves to clarify their testimony or determine a fact and isn't based on scientific or technical expertise. On the other hand, an expert has the specialized training, knowledge, experience, and expertise to provide evidence that is grounded in data and commonly held principles and methods.

For example, imagine that Local 282 member and Kraftwerk employee Morris C is heard slurring his words and speaking in a confrontational manner to his supervisor after returning from an extended lunch. The manager refers him for drug testing, and Morris C goes to Employee Health. The results of a breathalyzer test show that Morris C had a blood alcohol content of .07% an hour after he got back to the factory. He is terminated for being at work under the influence. Morris C denies it. The employer calls two witnesses. The supervisor says he witnessed Morris C stumbling around, slurring words, and that Morris smelled like alcohol or cleaning products. It's his opinion that Morris was drunk, which was why he referred him for testing. The other witness is an outside physician who worked in emergency medicine for 35 years before becoming a professional expert. Based on his medical training, 35 years of experience, and the scientific consensus that it takes one hour for blood alcohol content to go down .015%, he testifies that Morris C must have been legally drunk when he came back from lunch an hour before his test.

The supervisor is a layperson; the doctor is an expert. Before a witness is identified as an expert, the arbitrator and the other party may have questions about their education, skills, knowledge, expertise, and the basis of their testimony. If you want to call someone as a witness, be prepared to establish that expertise. Once a witness has been deemed "expert," they can testify about the facts of the case, even if they were not an eyewitness.

In some cases, a party will try to qualify a layperson as an expert witness. For example, the employer calls a corporate vice president to testify about how the company expects production standards to be met. That isn't an expert; that's just a lay witness explaining what the company policy is. The same can be said of the union steward who testifies about how the production standard is actually met. There's nothing wrong with either witness; they just aren't experts. They are testifying about the policy and practice at the plant. An expert might talk about industry standards or state and federal regulations.

Preparing the Witnesses

In a previous chapter, I suggested that you note the arbitrator's cancellation fee and schedule. Once you have your hearing date, note the cancellation date. A month before that date, start contacting witnesses to remind them about the hearing date, getting subpoenas, if necessary, and scheduling time to talk to the witnesses to prepare them for testifying.

A well-prepared advocate would enter all the dates on their calendar based on the hearing date, such as:

Hearing Date   March 17, 2020
Cancellation Date: February 25, 2020 (21 days before)
Start Case Prep: January 25, 2020

When you contact the witnesses, provide them with the hearing date, time, and location. Ask if they need a subpoena to testify or if they will appear on their own. Discuss how they plan to get to the hearing and confirm that their transportation is reliable. Set a time to discuss the topics they'll testify about and provide them with any documents they might have created, like emails, timecards, or witness statements.

Remember: If you don't have a subpoena, and they do not show up at the hearing, you either must proceed without them or request a continuance to subpoena them. Even friendly witnesses occasionally get embroiled in a work issue that they didn't anticipate. When in doubt, get a subpoena.

Witnesses will ask what time they will be called to testify. You may be able to provide a range of times. The party who has the burden of proof will go first, so the advocate could say, "in the morning," but it's hard to anticipate how long preliminary matters, arguments, and other witnesses will take. Remind witnesses to be flexible and available. If they can't be present all day, they should be no more than ten to fifteen minutes away. Most arbitrators will allow witnesses to appear by phone, and increasingly, video. As with other preparations, talking to the other side about scheduling witnesses or phone and video appearances before the day of hearing is always appreciated by the arbitrator and helps the hearing go more smoothly.

Practice Tips

- Select a hearing date as soon as reasonably possible after selecting the arbitrator, and calendar all the dates that relate to the hearing date, such as cancellation date and preparation time.
- Pull together documents for the hearing at least a month before the hearing. Make enough copies for the parties, the arbitrator, and the witnesses.
- Check in with witnesses after you've begun preparing the documents to confirm their availability and to prepare them for testifying.
- Request subpoenas with enough time to get the arbitrator's signature and serve the subpoenas on witnesses and the other party.
- Talk to the other side to prepare for the hearing. For example, the parties can prepare stipulations and joint exhibits, discuss witness scheduling and order, and decide on logistical arrangements.

CHAPTER 7
Arbitrability

Procedural Arbitrability

IT OCCASIONALLY HAPPENS that one party or the other challenges whether a dispute can be arbitrated. This is a question of "arbitrability," and there are two types: procedural and substantive. I will start by talking about Procedural Arbitrability.

As the name suggests, procedural arbitrability means that one party believes that there is a procedural error. Arbitrators and courts have held that it is up to the arbitrator to determine whether there is a procedural arbitrability issue.

The most common procedural arbitrability issue is timeliness. Timeliness concerns whether both parties have met the timeline required in their agreement. For example, the union might be required to file a grievance within ten days of learning about the incident that causes a dispute, and the employer might be required to respond to the grievance within seven days of receiving it. In most cases, arbitrators strictly enforce the timeline set out in the grievance procedure, where the parties have consistently enforced those requirements. As a general rule, **untimely grievances will not be heard.** Time limits are generally treated as jurisdictional; in other words, if the timeline wasn't met, the arbitrator doesn't have the authority to hear the merits of the case. This is less straightforward than it sounds.

Timelines must be consistently enforced. If the parties have been lax, or the practice has been inconsistent, the parties should be prepared to present evidence supporting their position about how the parties have treated timelines in the past. The employer might show that every grievance that was filed after ten days had passed was denied, while the union might show that the employer gave them a one-day grace period on many occasions in the past. The arbitrator will consider this evidence in deciding whether the grievance is arbitrable.

Timelines can be waived by mutual agreement. That's what happened in our example in Chapter 3. The union steward was on vacation when a union member was suspended and didn't return until after the deadline for filing the grievance had passed. He wrote the grievance and brought it to the supervisor, asking that the supervisor agree that the grievance be "deemed timely" because of his absence. The supervisor agreed, and they proceeded through the grievance procedure. At the arbitration hearing, a human resources manager testified that the supervisor had no authority to agree to waive the timeline and that the grievance was untimely when it was filed a few days late. I found that, if the supervisor had the authority to discipline employees and receive the grievance in the first place, he had the authority to agree to waive the timeline, and in fact, it was good for their labor relations that he did so. The discipline was upheld on the merits, and the union steward and supervisor continued to work together harmoniously to resolve disputes.

You probably noticed that my example contradicts the rule I stated: "Untimely grievances will not be heard" by an arbitrator.

Although the rule sounds firm, most arbitrators prefer to reach the merits and don't like to ding one party on a technicality. You sometimes hear this framed as, "Arbitrators dislike forfeiture," meaning they hate forcing one party to forfeit on minor grounds. Arbitrators typically find that a dispute is arbitrable if there is some ambiguity in the language.

When does the time to file a grievance start running? As with so many things, it depends on the contract. The most straightforward answer is, when the employee knew or should have known about the contract violation and has had a chance to raise it to their supervisor. If the contract language is unclear, an arbitrator isn't going to impose a timeline. However, an employer argument that the employee unreasonably delayed raising the issue after learning about it might have some merit.

What is "knew or should have known"? This depends entirely on the facts of the case. Obviously, an employee will probably know when they were terminated. On the other hand, an employee might not know that their vacation accrual is wrong until the union educates them about the contract. Parties seeking to enforce a strict timeline should show clear communication about the event triggering the grievance.

What about prospective events? An employer sends a notice on March 1 saying, effective June 1, they are unilaterally changing the schedule. When is the grievance ripe? When the event actually occurs. From March until the end of May, the union may seek to change the employer's mind and can hope to do so until it actually goes into effect. A grievance filed after June 1 within the timelines, is timely.

The deadline arrives when the contract says it does. But what happens if the deadline falls on a holiday or a Sunday? Again, this will depend on the facts and how the parties have treated those days in the past, but some arbitrators will apply state law court filing rules to this. For example, if the state law says that court filings that would be filed on a Monday, which is a state holiday, are still timely if filed the next day, an arbitrator might apply the same rule to the grievance filing deadline.

Another definition that an arbitrator might need clarification on is whether the parties use calendar days or business days. For example, a five-day deadline will have very different consequences if it's five calendar days rather than five business days. A union representative who isn't aware of the meaning of their own contract could very easily fail to file their grievance in a timely fashion.

It is precisely this type of problem that arbitrators see most often. Someone forgot, sent it a day or two late, sent it to the wrong person or made some other minor mistake that causes the grievance to be untimely. Human error is no excuse, if the timelines have been consistently enforced in the past. Again, any lax enforcement will probably excuse the human error, but it will be an evidentiary question.

Equitable Estoppel

An issue that sometimes arises in arbitration is a concept called "equitable estoppel." I'll try to keep this short, so you don't zone out or fall asleep. The quickest way to explain equitable estoppel is, **one party cannot lead the other party to believe that they agree or will resolve the issue, and then change course and claim the other side was untimely when they object to the failure to resolve the issue.** For example, there was a case where the employer agreed to pay contractual severance pay to the employees it was laying off and confirmed in writing several times that they would do this. They did not do this. The union tried to contact the employer about it and didn't hear back until the employer's bankruptcy attorney told the union that the employer would not pay. The union filed a grievance, and the employer claimed the grievance was outside the 3-day window for filing after the employees received their final paychecks. The arbitrator rejected that timeliness argument, saying the union didn't affirmatively know the employees wouldn't get it until the bankruptcy lawyer told them so. It was reasonable to believe, based on the employer's earlier statements, that they'd get the money.

The moral of the story is, arbitrators don't like it when the parties try to play tricks and are unlikely to find the grievance is not arbitrable if the side arguing for lack of arbitrability was playing games during the grievance procedure.

Continuing Violations

Continuing violations grievances are another exception to the idea that untimely grievances will not be arbitrated. In a continuing violation grievance, the union alleges that the violation of the collective bargaining agreement recurs, maybe on a daily or weekly basis. Every day is a new violation, and therefore a grievance is not untimely even if it's filed outside the time limits of the first violation. The remedy may be restricted to the time frame of the grievance. For example, a group of workers believed that they should have been paid on-call pay rather than standby pay when one of them reads the contract and decides that having to wait at the workplace, as they have done for years, sounds more than like on-call than standby as those terms are defined by the contract. The employer says, "Nope, your grievance is untimely, there's a past practice, etc., etc." The arbitrator will probably disagree with that employer and find that the allegation is timely, but she will likely limit the recovery to thirty days (or some other contractual limit) prior to filing the grievance, if she finds that a violation has occurred.

Substantive Arbitrability

Substantive arbitrability differs from procedural in that it depends on the question of whether the arbitrator has the authority to decide on the underlying substantive issue. For example, a contract may state that an arbitrator may not hear cases of a certain type. Substantive arbitrability issues can be raised to the arbitrator, but they are also raised after an arbitration decision in court when one party (or both) feels that the arbitrator exceeded their powers under the collective bargaining agreement.

These are cases in which one party believes the arbitrator doesn't have jurisdiction over the subject matter. One example of this is Last Chance Agreements, which is a broader topic, but in general, LCAs limit the arbitrator's jurisdiction to deciding whether the employee violated the terms of the LCA or not. If the employee did, the consequence is spelled out in the LCA, and the arbitrator cannot alter the outcome.

Managers frequently assert "management rights" as the basis for why an arbitrator cannot hear a dispute. The actual language of the agreement will be very important here and will involve a lot of argument. As a practice tip, both sides will need to identify what specific language in the agreement gives, or does not give, the arbitrator jurisdiction to hear the case.

Another substantive arbitrability issue arises when a party adds a claim or theory to the original grievance when they get to hearing. Just as an employee has a right to know what they are being fired for, an employer has a right to know what the union believes the contract violation is.

Often there is language in the agreement that limits the arbitrator's jurisdiction, such as "cannot add to, subtract from or modify the agreement." If one party believes that the remedy sought by the other side would do that, such as asking an arbitrator to create a new attendance policy, then they should argue this language prevents such a remedy, and ask that if a violation be found, the parties be ordered to fashion their own remedy, for example. In addition, parties sometimes ask arbitrators to act as EEOC administrators, or workers comp judges, or want a legal ruling on a statute. At the end of the day, the arbitrator is there to hear contract disputes and usually wants to hear only those.

Finally, when should the parties argue the arbitrability issues? As soon as possible, not only in the grievance procedure but in the hearing. Some parties request bifurcation—that is, they want the arbitrator to hear the arbitrability issue before they hear the merits of the case. Unless the parties agree to bifurcate, the arbitrator retains the jurisdiction to rule on bifurcation. Often to an arbitrator, it makes more sense to hear the whole case at once, since the arbitrability issues are often interwoven, but it depends on the facts of the case.

Practice Tips

- Procedural arbitrability issues, like timeliness or continuing violations, are decided by an arbitrator.
- Substantive arbitrability issues may be raised to an arbitrator or brought to court.
- An untimely grievance will not be heard, except when it will!
- Raise arbitrability issues early in the grievance procedure.
- The decision of whether to bifurcate can be made jointly by the parties or raised to the arbitrator.

CHAPTER 8
Opening Statement

Preliminary Matters

IT's THE DAY of the hearing, and it's time to get started. What comes first? Surprisingly, it's not the opening statement. Before the arbitrator starts the hearing, she usually asks several questions off the record. She'll ask the same questions on the record in a few moments, but it's useful to have some preliminary information. Here are the questions I commonly ask at the beginning of a hearing:

1. Have all the steps of the grievance procedure been met or waived?
2. Is the matter properly before me, and will my decision be final and binding?
3. Do you want me to retain jurisdiction over the remedy if that becomes necessary?
4. Is there a statement of the issue?
5. Are there any stipulated facts or joint exhibits?

Once I know the answers to these questions, I start the hearing. If there is a court reporter, I say, "Let's go on the record." If the parties' answers to my questions were short and sweet, I might summarize their views and ask for their agreement. If they have some argument they want to make about the procedural issues, I invite them to answer the question on the record so that their position is preserved.

We mark exhibits, if necessary, and identify any arbitrability issues that we will be addressing during the hearing. I confirm who has the burden of proof and invite them to make an opening statement.

Burden of Proof

Burden of proof is the concept that the party who initiated the action bears the responsibility for demonstrating that the evidence warrants finding in their favor. In a discipline case, the employer has the burden of proof. In a contract interpretation case, the union has the burden of proof.

How much evidence is needed depends on the forum. For example, in a criminal case, the prosecutor must demonstrate that the defendant committed the criminal act "beyond a reasonable doubt." However, in labor arbitration, the burden of proof is "preponderance of the evidence."

A preponderance of the evidence means that the facts show that it is more likely than not that the accused behavior occurred. You might say it's fifty percent plus one if you were placing the evidence on an actual scale.

The party who has the burden of proof gets to make the first opening statement because it's their case to make. The opposing party may make an opening statement after the first party has made theirs or may reserve until after the moving party has put on their evidence. Arbitrators are split about whether they require an opening statement from the opposing party. Some require it because they want to know both sides of the case before they hear evidence. I have no preference and am aware that some parties use it tactically, reserving their opening statement in order to address the actual facts that arise rather than the arguments that the moving party made. In some cases, that tactic works. In others, it makes the opposing party seem unprepared, as though they weren't certain what arguments to make at the outset, so they waited until they'd learned the case. As an opposing party, consider how your choice might affect the arbitrator's view of your arguments.

Finally, the Opening Statement

The opening statement should be basic. The advocate should answer the issue, state the standard, and say what evidence they will introduce to support that conclusion. State all your best arguments and identify what evidence you believe will come into the record to support those arguments. The advocate should also say what remedy the arbitrator should order if she agrees with their position.

Here's a Mad Libs style opening statement on a discharge case:

"Good morning. We believe that the evidence will demonstrate that the employer had just cause to discharge Joseph Ramone from his position as a forklift operator at our Rockaway Beach facility. On [DATE], Mr. Ramone [VERB] in violation of [POLICY, RULE OR PROCEDURE]. The supervisor will testify that [FACTS] and [NUMBER] eyewitnesses will testify that [FACTS]. This isn't the first time Mr. Ramone has been subject to discipline. He had a [DISCIPLINE] in [YEAR] and [DISCIPLINE] in [YEAR]. Therefore, there was progressive discipline that was not effective at correcting Mr. Ramone's behavior. The Union will argue [LIST ARGUMENTS YOU ANTICIPATE AND OFFER REBUTTAL]. For these reasons, we ask that you deny the grievance and uphold the discharge."

Obviously there are many cases that will require more information, such as the nature of the work or the kinds of policies in effect. Unless the other side is willing to stipulate to every fact in your opening statement, it isn't necessary to identify every piece of information you will be relying on to build the case. That's the point of the hearing.

The reasons why "short and sweet" is better than "long and rambling" should be obvious, but let me spell them out anyway. You do not want to bore or confuse the arbitrator right off the bat. You also don't want to promise something you can't deliver. For example, if you promise there's an eyewitness to the grievant's misdeeds, and that person doesn't show up or doesn't testify exactly as you've promised, it undermines the persuasiveness of your case. One advocate explained it to me this way: "You need to tell the arbitrator what your case is about (opening statement), then show the arbitrator what the case is about (evidence), and then tell them again one last time (closing statement)."

The opposing party should make a similarly brief and thoughtful opening statement, laying out all the reasons why the moving party's evidence isn't as strong as it sounds, and sharing facts that might be mitigating or persuasive. Finally, it's important to state the opposing party's sought-after remedy, so the arbitrator knows exactly what you want.

Practice Tips

- Be prepared to handle procedural questions at the beginning of the hearing.
- Know who has the burden of proof and tailor your opening statements to answer the specific issue in the case.
- Don't make claims you cannot support.
- Be prepared to make your opening statement at the beginning of the hearing, even if you prefer not to. It's up to the arbitrator whether you can reserve your argument.
- Keep it simple.

CHAPTER 9
Evidence in Arbitration

Material, Relevant, and Competent Evidence

ONE REASON THAT non-lawyer advocates are leery of doing their own arbitrations is that they worry they are not familiar enough with the rules of evidence to be effective in a hearing. They may believe that law school imparts some advantage. It's true that every law student is required to take evidence and that it's tested on the bar exam of every state. What many advocates do not realize, however, is that the formal rules of evidence are not required in arbitration.

Remember, the purpose of arbitration is to be a fast, fair, and economical method of resolving workplace disputes. The parties shouldn't be bogged down in discovery and evidentiary motions about what will be considered by the arbitrator.

The rules of evidence do play some role in the arbitration hearing. Some might argue that the formal rules of evidence migrated into the arbitration process because lawyers got involved and wanted to be seen as having an advantage in that process because of their formal education. A less cynical view is that the rules of evidence also help the arbitrator determine the value of the information being presented.

In other words, the Rules of Evidence are present in an arbitration, but they do not govern the process. What comes into the record may differ from what the arbitrator ultimately considers when making a decision. For example, a trial judge might prohibit hearsay, while an arbitrator may permit it, but still won't consider it as the truth. It's a fine line that advocates understand better as they gain experience.

Ultimately, arbitrators are looking for evidence that is material, relevant, and competent. Information that meets those three criteria often forms the basis of the factual understanding that the arbitrator has about the case.

Material evidence is **reasonably related to an issue in the case** being heard. If a witness testifies about the weather, it may be the reason for the grievant's absence. Otherwise, it wouldn't be material. If evidence is not permitted by the CBA or the law, it is immaterial to the case. Some CBAs prohibit discipline records that predate a certain time period. Some states have laws prohibiting the admission of unemployment claim information in any hearing. In those cases, the old discipline records and the unemployment claim information would not be material, and an arbitrator would not admit it into the record.

Relevant evidence is information **that tends to prove the issue** to which it is directed. The distinction between material and relevant is narrow but real. A material fact may or may not prove something, while a relevant fact tends to prove that thing. Let's take the weather as an example. Grievant Neil Purt claims that he missed work on February 3 because his car skidded off the road while driving in the rain, and he had to wait for a tow truck and the insurance adjuster before he could get to work. Kraftwerk's attorney enters evidence that the weather forecast that day was sunny and dry, so Neil must be lying. That is material evidence that relates to an issue in the case.

Local 282's attorney produces photographs from the accident site that were taken by the adjuster and provided to Neil. The adjuster testifies that he took the pictures and kept them with the file but does not remember this particular case. The photos show that the car is wet and that there was a large puddle on the road. The photograph is date- and time- stamped on the day that Neil says he had his accident, which is also the day he was absent. This is material evidence (relates to an issue) and relevant evidence (tends to prove that Neil was telling the truth).

Finally, the evidence must be competent. "Competent" refers to the nature of the information source, and usually refers to a witness. Witnesses that are considered to be "incompetent" are young children, people whose mental impairment prevents them from recalling information or from understanding an oath to tell the truth, or someone who has been ruled "incompetent" by a court. Certain legal privileges that prevent testifying may also render someone "incompetent" to testify even if they are perfectly competent people. For example, clergy privilege or spousal privilege may prevent a pastor or wife from testifying.

Sometimes unions will argue there is a union representative privilege that is akin to the attorney-client privilege which protects communications between the union rep and their member. Arbitrators differ to a certain degree about this privilege, but there are quite a few who agree that a union representative's discussions about legal or bargaining strategy with a grievant or group of members should be given the same level of privilege as a lawyer in the same or similar situation.

Direct and Circumstantial Evidence

Trial courts distinguish between direct evidence and circumstantial evidence. If you were to rely solely on TV court dramas to understand the distinction, you would believe that direct evidence is "better than" circumstantial evidence. This isn't true; either can be used to prove a fact.

Direct evidence is proof which, if believed, proves a factual claim regardless of other evidence. If there was a killer who admitted his crime, and witnesses who testified that they saw him kill the victim, then that's direct evidence, even if some other person claimed to have done it, assuming you believe the killer and the witnesses. Direct evidence must be persuasive; the finder of fact (here, the arbitrator) must be persuaded that it is true.

Circumstantial evidence is a combination of persuasive facts which, when taken together, leave only one reasonable factual conclusion. With circumstantial evidence, you must prove every step of the chain of events. Circumstantial evidence of the killer's actions might include drops of the victim's blood on his car, no alibi for the time of the murder, a recent gun purchase. The standard in a criminal case is "beyond a reasonable doubt," so in that case, the jury would need to find that the combination of those facts, taken together, leave only the reasonable, factual conclusion that our man was the killer.

Once you've established the circumstantial evidence, and the evidence survives attack, the arbitrator is as apt to rely on circumstantial evidence as they are to rely on direct evidence. In a less dramatic arbitration example, the company charges Bonnie Jonjovi with time theft when they discover that she is walking into the building thirty minutes after the start of her shift, but she's already been clocked in for the entire time. Bonnie claims that she clocked in and went back out to her car, but the supervisor is certain she didn't see Bonnie that morning. The day before, Bonnie was overheard saying she loved to party all the time, and "if I roll in late, you got me, sis?" to her friend. The employer argues that this combination of facts proves that Bonnie had her friend clock in for her. The union argues that the employer hasn't met their burden of proof.

It's not clear whether this combination of facts, if proven, lead to only one reasonable factual conclusion. Both direct evidence and circumstantial evidence can be attacked in the following ways:

- Question the reliability of the source
- Present contradictory evidence
- Challenge the validity of one or more underlying facts
- Prove additional facts
- Use the evidence to prove an exculpatory explanation.

With these tools, both parties have a lot of opportunity for attacking the evidence presented by the other side. Either Bonnie or the supervisor might be discredited. Another witness, like Bonnie's friend or another coworker, may have a different recollection. There might be security footage somewhere. Bonnie's watch may have stopped. Who knows? A thorough investigation will turn up evidence both good and bad, and it's the advocate's responsibility to use that evidence to tell a true story that persuades the arbitrator that their side is the most reasonable, factual, credible way to understand the issue.

Direct Examination

For new practitioners, examining witnesses is one of the most daunting aspects of presenting a case. Even many experienced advocates find examining witnesses to be stressful. Fortunately, there are dozens of other books that can walk you through the details of how to do an effective witness examination. The best book on the topic is *Effective Direct & Cross Examination* by John Keker & William Brockett ($219, CEB). If the price tag is too high, you can easily find a copy in your local Law Library.

The best way to tackle direct examination is to prepare your questions ahead of time. If you use those questions to prepare your witness, you can fine-tune them and note the expected answers. On direct examination, your questions should elicit a story from the witness. The witness should talk much more than you do. Your question should not provide the answer—the witness should. Limit your questions to only the topics your witness has knowledge of. Their answers should never be guesses or speculation. Be careful if you use hypothetical questions. Hypothetical questions should be grounded in knowledge and experience they've shown to have.

Sometimes a witness will provide a vague answer. You may need to clarify for them that you are asking for an estimate, not a guess. The distinction between an estimate and a guess is best explained by referring to something concrete that they can observe. I can estimate the length of the table that I am sitting at; I would be guessing if I tried to tell you the length of the table in your dining room.

While it is great to be prepared with written questions, it's also important to listen to your witness' answers. They may say something different than you expect. Their answer may need a follow-up question to elicit more information, or you may need to have them clarify their answer. Don't be so wed to your prepared questions that you miss a chance to make a clearer record.

In other words, don't overprepare. Direct examination should be conversational. The witness should feel at ease, and your demeanor will contribute to that.

Each witness should only testify about the particular area they know. The foundation for facts that are not in dispute only needs to be given once. For example, every management witness does not need to describe the history of the company unless it's actually disputed by the union. It may not even be necessary at all. The only facts that are needed at arbitration hearing are relevant facts that are material to the dispute.

Cross Examination: What Not to Do

As a labor arbitrator and hearing officer, I've listened to dozens, if not hundreds, of witnesses being cross-examined. In legal training, there's a lot of focus on how to examine a witness. Baby lawyers learn how to ask a direct question versus a leading question, how to lay a foundation, and how to craft a question to avoid objections.

There are great books and programs that teach people examination skills, but they don't spend much time on the tone that a lawyer should deploy to effectively cross-exam a witness, so lawyers learn some of their tricks from television. This leads to all kinds of theatrics: escalating aggression, gotcha questions, and fake sarcasm are always on tap.

I might be the first neutral to say this, but these theatrics don't work. Here are my top tips for tactics you should avoid if you want the arbitrator to trust your cross-examination.

Don't Punch Down

Most witnesses have never testified under oath before. They're nervous, and the whole format of testifying feels stilted and alien. There's someone typing everything they're saying, and two lawyers are arguing about their words before they can even answer a question. Many times, they are testifying because of a subpoena, or because their employer has requested that they appear. All this is to say, they aren't usually willing participants in the hearing.

It drives me crazy when the opposing attorney, someone the witness has never met, employs bullying tactics against a witness. It's especially irritating when the witness was either subordinate to their client in some way or are obviously not familiar with the legal environment the lawyer swims in. When a lawyer beats up on a person like that, the neutral feels protective of the witness or causes the neutral to want to intervene to change the tone of the examination. While the attorney may feel like that's not appropriate or fair, it's a natural reaction of a neutral to de-escalate situations. We are in favor of learning the truth, not destroying someone because their memory doesn't benefit the attorney's client.

Neutrals try not to draw adverse conclusions about the case from this behavior, but attorneys should recognize when the line of questioning suggests arguments that might not favor their client, such as an indication that the client supports excessive aggression towards or mistreatment of subordinate individuals.

Don't Manufacture Credibility Issues

First-person eyewitness testimony is gold standard evidence in hearings, but it's also a historical artifact of the English system. By the time issues get to a fact hearing, most people's memories have faded or gotten confused, and the emotions they felt at the time of the incident often cloud their recollection. For example, a man wielding a knife in Times Square was apprehended by a police officer. Multiple witnesses reported that the police officer had used a gun to subdue the man, but video evidence showed that the police officer had not drawn her weapon. Her testimony and the photographs taken at the time supported the fact that her gun stayed in its snapped-tight enclosure. But witnesses couldn't shake their beliefs about what they had seen because it was a very stressful event that happened in a crowded place.

When a witness does not remember perfectly the events that occurred long prior, attorneys should not treat this witness as a liar. Neutrals are aware that memory degrades, testimony can be suggested, and that witnesses are trying to please their questioner, even if they are adversarial. When a lawyer acts as though a memory problem is a lie, that doesn't impeach the witness. In fact, it feels like bullying again, and it doesn't look good for the lawyer.

Here is an example of a cross-examination I recently witnessed.

Attorney: How many staff members were in the room that day?

Witness: I'm not sure, I remember me and Dawn, and there were more people by the end, but I don't know the number.

Attorney: I need you to estimate how many staff were in the room that day, please.

Witness: I really can't say. Maybe five?

Attorney: Who were they?

Witness: Again, I can't really remember. It was more than two years ago.

Attorney: Are you covering for someone?

This question is intended as an attack on the character's witness and not designed to elicit useful information. Therefore, it shouldn't be used. There are effective ways of impeaching a witness (that is, demonstrating that they are not truthful) that do not involve character attacks. Besides, who has ever answered "Yes" to the question, "Are you a liar?"

Don't Go on a Fishing Expedition

Sometimes lawyers don't know what to ask a witness. They may have prepared some questions, but they aren't sure what the witness is going to say at the hearing. This is more common in administrative hearings and arbitrations where there haven't been any depositions, but there's no reason that you can't anticipate the areas that each witness will address, and which documents they might be asked to discuss. On more than one occasion, I've seen lawyers flip through piles of exhibits, asking random questions about the facts to see if they can elicit some information that might damage the other party's case. To the neutral, this doesn't look like Perry Mason, it looks like a lack of preparation. Not every witness needs to be cross-examined about every single fact. The best lawyers limit their questions to reinforce the arguments they intend to make. It isn't uncommon for good lawyers to not cross-examine a witness at all.

Don't Invent Conspiracy Theories

Occasionally an attorney will spin a defense that involves blaming a whole group of other people or organizations for collaborating in the destruction of their client. While fraud and conspiracy are real criminal offenses, they are rarely the cause of their client's bad situation. As with the example of manufactured credibility that I gave above, alluding to elaborate schemes meant to frame a client is not an effective strategy for convincing the neutral that your client's story is the one they should believe. Most neutrals have an "Occam's razor" view of their cases, meaning that the most straightforward explanation is probably the one that fits. It's important that all of your questions point toward a straightforward story, and not a ruse concocted by five other people and the Deep State.

Which is not to say that sometimes, people aren't out to get their client. I have seen plenty of cases where the supervisor and the person's coworkers did not like an employee, so everything that the employee did was interpreted in a negative way, and they were never given the benefit of the doubt in the way other people might have been. If that's the story, tell that story. If the employee is not well-liked, is treated differently, and is being retaliated against for speaking up, you have a straightforward story that a neutral will understand and is likely to be elicited from coworkers on cross-examination.

Don't Enumerate Their Failings

Witnesses are there to testify about the events that form the basis of the issue before the neutral. They aren't there to be reminded of their personnel records, their divorces, their mental health issues, or their criminal records. The only relevant former misconduct that should be raised in cross-examination concerns truthfulness. If they were terminated for lying or have perjured themselves in some other proceeding, then that's relevant to their truthfulness. Otherwise, leave the skeletons in the closet.

Don't Ask the Same Questions Over and Over Again

If a witness doesn't remember something, or they gave an answer that your client doesn't like, I can guarantee you that asking the question repeatedly isn't going to refresh their memory or cause them to change their answer. More likely, the repeated questions will annoy the neutral and aggravate opposing counsel, who will draw you into a series of arguments that make you seem like you don't understand what their witness is saying. Make your record and get out. If you don't like what they said, move on and hope no one remembers it. They will, but it won't sting as much if you don't pound it into their heads.

Objections

Objections are used to draw attention to evidence that the objecting party believes should not be a part of the evidentiary record. They are invoked during witness testimony or when a document is being introduced. Here are the basic objections that I encounter in arbitration.

1. Lacks foundation: This objection is used when a question to a witness assumes a fact that has not been introduced before. It can also be used when a document has been introduced but not identified. If you get this objection, your best course of action may be to back up and ask a few preliminary questions of the witness rather than arguing about it with the other side.

2. Compound: This objection is used when the question has two or more parts and doesn't call for a single answer. Again, the best course of action is to ask two or more separate questions that lead the witness to the same conclusion.

3. Vague: This objection is used when the answer could relate to different things, such as different occurrences. If the question was in fact vague, like, "What did he say?" then just back up and ask a more specific question. If the question made sense in the context of a series of questions, and the objection is being asserted to interrupt your train of thought, don't let it get to you. Either wait for the arbitrator to rule, or just go ahead and rephrase the question in a way that includes additional

information and makes clear that the objecting party wasn't paying attention or something.

4. Calls for a conclusion: I hear this objection most often when the moving party wants their union president or the top manager to say what the outcome of the arbitration should be. For example, "Did you have just cause to terminate Jerry?" or "Did the employer violate the contract when he denied Jerry his band practice leave?" These questions and the inevitable objections make me roll my eyes internally. Of course, the manager thinks they had just cause, and the union president thinks the contract was violated. I also know that the ultimate decision rests with me, and I'm not persuaded by the obvious opinion of the party witness.

5. Argumentative: This objection relates to questions that are really just arguments with the witness. They often take the form of repeated leading questions and have the feel of a bad Perry Mason impression. As I discussed in my section on cross-examination, I am not impressed by arguments with a witness. If an advocate is making a more general point about an issue in the case and the way the matter has been treated historically, I will allow the question, but badgering and arguing aren't useful for soliciting useful facts.

6. Hearsay: This is the most complex of the objections and warrants a longer discussion.

Hearsay is an out-of-court statement. It is any statement made by a person who is not testifying at the hearing. Any time a sworn witness wants to tell an arbitrator what someone else said, that's hearsay.

Simple enough, right? How could something as straightforward as that—hearsay—be one of the thorniest issues for new advocates, even folks who went to law school.

When a witness is testifying in court, they are not allowed to share hearsay. The complication is that there are so many exceptions to that rule that the admissibility of hearsay becomes a huge matter of contention at trials.

In arbitration, we make it easier. Hearsay is generally admitted. Parties don't need to remember every exception to the hearsay rule. That doesn't mean the arbitrator considers it when making her decision. In fact, most arbitrators personally apply a "no hearsay" rule when they are formulating their decisions. They will not rely on an out-of-court statement to establish a fact.

As a practical matter, it still makes sense to state a hearsay objection to a statement or document which was created by someone other than the person testifying. The objection gives the parties an opportunity to explain to the arbitrator what purpose the evidence serves.

How to Use the Rules of Evidence

Even if you did not go to law school, you can use the rules of evidence to prepare and present your case. While preparing your case, apply the guidelines I've described in this chapter to each fact you intend to prove.

1. Is the fact material and relevant?
2. Is the source of the fact (the witness or document) competent?
3. Are your witnesses and documents credible and original?
4. Have you anticipated hearsay issues and considered why they might still be relied upon?
5. If you don't have an original witness to the event, such as the decision-maker, how will you establish that the new witness is capable of testifying to the events?

If your evidence passes through these questions unscathed in your preparation, you are unlikely to be derailed by any objections from the other side.

At the hearing, the rules of evidence can be used in a different way: to object to the introduction of evidence by the other side. If you are attuned to hearsay and familiar with the rules I've described, you can object to the admission of the evidence, drawing the arbitrator's attention to the weakness of their case. A word of warning, however: Use objections sparingly and correctly. Don't repeat them to the same piece of evidence once the arbitrator has ruled. Make your point and get out.

CHAPTER 10
Closing Arguments

LOSING ARGUMENTS CAN be made orally at the end of the hearing or in writing as a legal brief or letter. Closing arguments should closely resemble the opening statement with one critical difference. Instead of describing the party's view of the events that led to the grievance, the closing argument should refer to the actual evidence that came in at hearing. How do the testimony and documents that are in the record support your party's position?

The closing argument is also an opportunity to describe to the arbitrator why some evidence is stronger than other evidence. Stronger evidence is material, relevant, and competent. Remember, you are trying to convince the arbitrator that the evidence in the case leads to the factual conclusion that you are seeking.

At the same time, do not ignore evidence that is unfavorable to your case. Arbitrators are aware of the weaknesses in your case and are interested in knowing how you would explain them. Perhaps a witness for your case could not recall a crucial detail, and you know the opposing side will argue that the witness is lying or that the detail did not occur. There are several ways to address this.

"Tom Lee testified that he was Bill Joel's supervisor at the time of the incident. Although he did not recall at the hearing that he witnessed Mr. Joel sleeping in the breakroom, he confirmed that his signature was on his witness statement. Employer's Exhibit 7. More than a year has elapsed since the events; it's not surprising that Mr. Lee doesn't remember every detail."

It's important to remember that the burden of proof is a preponderance of the evidence. Are the facts on your side more persuasive than the facts on the other side? If the case were cut and dried, it probably wouldn't have gone to arbitration. Review the arguments that the other side made at the hearing and during the grievance procedure and address them in your closing argument.

Don't shy away from the good arguments that the other side makes. It's more persuasive to concede their point and offer your solution or answer to the issue they've raised. An employer may need to explain why an employee with many years of service with the employer has been discharged without prior warning. Acknowledge the years of service and note the actions were serious enough to overcome that seniority. On the other side, the union should acknowledge the severity of the problem but point to the employee's contrite testimony as evidence the problem won't recur.

The closing argument is also the last chance to tell the arbitrator what remedy you want and what remedy you could live with. It is often at the very end of the argument that one party concedes that a long-term suspension would be acceptable, or that a back pay remedy could be limited to thirty days. Slipping in alternate remedy proposals helps the arbitrator think more expansively than a straight win-lose decision. On the other hand, if a certain remedy is totally unacceptable, you can make that known as well. You may not win, but at least the arbitrator knows the stakes of their decision.

Practice Tips

- Prepare your closing argument based on your opening statement, referring to the evidence that actually came at the hearing.
- Identify the acceptable remedies and articulate them in your closing argument.

CHAPTER 11
What Comes Next

The Decision

O NCE THE HEARING has concluded and arguments have been made, the matter is "submitted" to the arbitrator. The parties now wait for their decision. In most cases, you should expect to receive a decision within ninety days. Many arbitrators strive to complete a decision within thirty days, but it's dependent on the volume of their caseload generally whether they can review the entire record and write a decision that quickly.

Some CBAs say that an arbitrator must render a decision within a certain time frame, and if the parties want to enforce that time frame, they are well-advised to let the arbitrator know before they begin the hearing, in case the arbitrator cannot complete it within that time frame. Alternately, the parties can advise the arbitrator of the time frame and ask that the decision be completed as reasonably close to that time as possible. Some arbitrators insist that timelines for their decision be waived.

In some cases, a decision will take longer than ninety days, and it puts the parties in a bind. I recommend that the parties discuss between them how to proceed and that one advocate reach out to the arbitrator on behalf of both parties, preferably by email with a copy to the other side, asking when the parties might expect a decision and if there's anything more the arbitrator needs to complete their work. If the arbitrator has an assistant, you might include them in the correspondence to see whether something has happened that explains the delay.

If that doesn't work, reach out to the appointing agency to let them know that the decision is delayed. If the arbitrator was a private selection and not appointed from a roster, then reach out to a professional association that the arbitrator belongs to, such as the National Academy of Arbitrators, to find out if something has gone wrong, Perhaps the arbitrator has suffered a medical problem that is causing the delay.

Arbitrators are encouraged by the Academy and the roster agencies to have succession plans in place if they are not able to complete their work. Not every arbitrator does, of course, so it occasionally falls to the parties to find another arbitrator to assist in resolving the matter. Hopefully, this is so rare that few of my readers ever encounter that problem.

Publication

When the decision comes, it will be accompanied by a bill. Please pay it.

Some arbitrators also include a request that the parties allow them to submit the decision for publication. In my experience, the losing party often objects, while the winning party agrees. Because the arbitrator cannot ethically submit their decision for publication without the consent of both parties, the decision doesn't get published. This is unfortunate. Published decisions are one way for unions and employers to learn about cases and the arbitrator's approach to their novel issue.

Most arbitrators and publishers are happy to redact identifying names of the grievants and witnesses, and publication is limited to readers of a dwindling number of labor law guides. The temporary embarrassment of losing doesn't outweigh the value to other unions and employers of learning about the arbitrator's approach to cases.

If publication were more common and accepted, there would be more information upon which the parties could base their own decisions. Knowing that a vast majority of arbitrators disagree with one side might encourage settlement or withdrawal.

Next time an arbitrator asks if their decision might be submitted for publication, ask whether it could be edited or redacted for publication to limit exposure of information about your organization, rather than refusing outright. Your decision could help modernize labor law.

CHAPTER 12
Other Kinds of Arbitration and ADR

Expedited Arbitration

As its name suggests, expedited arbitration is a process that streamlines the arbitration hearing and results in a quick decision. Different parties negotiate different kinds of expedited arbitration. I'll describe two forms that I've observed or participated in.

Example 1: A large corporation with multiple locations and a unionized workforce had a huge backlog of grievances after a long strike and difficult bargaining. The parties each designated a representative, and those two people sat with an arbitrator to figure out which grievances would be sent to expedited arbitration. The rest of the grievances were settled or withdrawn. The parties then reserved two days a month with the arbitrator. On hearing day, the party representatives and the arbitrator acted as a panel to hearing four grievances, two in the morning and two in the afternoon. Legal counsel gave factual opening statements, and all facts were assumed to be accurate and agreed upon by the parties. In other words, they were stipulated unless there was an actual dispute. Witnesses were called only if there was a factual dispute. As a practical matter, this meant that the grievant and the supervisor usually testified. After short closing remarks, the panel met in executive session and then issued an opinion reflecting the majority view of the panel. Once the backlog was dealt with, the parties decided to keep arbitrating in this manner because it was so much more effective for them.

Example 2: A large, unionized public sector employer uses a similar expedited process for three of its bargaining units. However, the expedited process is only used for discipline up to a fifteen-day suspension or discharge for attendance issues. That panel schedules eight to ten cases a day once per month. The party representatives give their opinion in an executive session and are occasionally able to settle cases between them. When they do not, the arbitrator issues a verbal decision called a "bench" decision.

Expedited arbitration makes sense for large employers who have mature labor relations and lots of grievances. In both cases, the parties are represented either by in-house counsel or human resources and union staff, further reducing costs.

Public Sector ADR

In the public sector, there are several types of alternative dispute resolution. I'll describe a few that I'm familiar with from practicing California; other states have similar procedures.

Civil Service Hearings: Many counties in California have civil service commissions, each of which has a different mandate and scope of authority. In general, they have authority over county employees. Some commissions delegate decision-making authority to arbitrators. Others hear discipline cases themselves. A third approach is to retain arbitrators, or hearing officers, to hold a hearing and write a recommended decision on discipline that the commission can accept or reject.

Fact Finding: California public sector labor law has established a process called "fact finding" for public sector unions and employers who have reached an impasse in bargaining. Once the parties have declared an impasse, they attempt to mediate the issues. If mediation is not successful, a "fact-finding panel" holds a hearing to hear about each party's proposals and the basis for their positions. The panel consists of a union representative, an employer representative, and a neutral chairperson. After the hearing, the panel may discuss possible settlement opportunities. If that isn't successful, the neutral chairperson writes a Fact-Finding Report that includes recommendations for settlement. The report is advisory, but it remains confidential for ten days to permit the parties to resume bargaining if they choose. If they do not reach a settlement within ten days, the report becomes public, and the employer may impose their last, best, and final offer.

Mediation

Mediation is an effort to settle a dispute with the help of a neutral mediator. I recommend selecting a mediator who has knowledge of labor relations when trying to settle grievances. Otherwise, you'll find much of your time is spent educating the mediator rather than discussing settlement.

Mediation is confidential, and the parties may meet privately (or "ex parte") with the mediator to discuss their case and possible settlement opportunities. Settlement discussions and other work that comes out of mediation (like proposed settlement terms or language) are not admissible at arbitration.

Some lawyers or union reps find it useful to have their client or union member hear the mediator's view of the strengths and weaknesses of their case.

Many states and the federal government have free or low-cost mediation available, and many arbitrators conduct mediations as well. If you select an arbitrator for mediation, be aware that most will not accept an appointment as arbitrator for that same case at a later date. Arbitrators serve a different role at arbitration and seek to keep that distinction clear.

Final Words and Acknowledgments

I HOPE THIS BOOK gives you the tools you need to deepen your labor arbitration practice. Labor arbitrators genuinely view themselves as advocates for workplace justice and want to assist unions and employers in strengthening their industry and the workers within that industry. Collective bargaining truly is the best way to grow strong companies, good unions, and loyal employees. I am fortunate to play a role in strengthening those relationships and sharing my expertise with the next generation of union representatives, human resources specialists, and lawyers.

Please let me know what you think about my book by visiting my website (www.andreadooleyarbitration.com) or sending me an email (andrealdooley@gmail.com).

I'd like to thank the people whose support and feedback was vital to this project: Dan Altemus, William Clayton, Peter Dahlens, and Anne Janks. Their professional expertise and understanding of my project improved it tremendously. All mistakes are mine! I also give begrudging acknowledgment to the COVID-19 pandemic, without which I would not have had time to finish this book! This book is dedicated to Bill Sokol, who told me to stop touching my hair but in every other way encouraged me to do whatever I wanted in arbitration and the world, and to Gerald McKay, who brought his humor and creativity to bear on complex labor issues to the benefit of everyone who appeared before him.

www.ingramcontent.com/pod-product-compliance
Lightning Source LLC
Chambersburg PA
CBHW071111210326
41519CB00020B/6256